Let's Learn About…
Things to Drive!

Curious Toddler Series

Volume 3

Cheryl Shireman

ISBN: 1477534709
ISBN-13: 978-1477534700

DEDICATION

This book is dedicated to Anna Lee - my favorite toddler.

With much love, Bomb Bomb

Some things to drive are big.

Some things to drive are small.

Boys can learn to drive
things.

Girls can learn to drive things
too.

Some cars carry families.

Some cars go fast on
racetracks!

A passenger bus carries people
to many places.

A school bus carries children to school.

Some airplanes are very big
and carry many people.

Some airplanes are smaller
and only carry a few people.

Trains are very big and have
loud horns.

Trains run on railroad tracks.

Some motorcycles have two wheels.

Some motorcycles have four
wheels.

Snowmobiles travel across the snow.

Jet skis travel across the water.

Some things, like bulldozers,
push dirt.

Some things, like backhoes,
dig in the dirt.

Pickup trucks often carry things.

Semi-trucks can carry many things.

Some trucks carry mail.

Some trucks carry dirt or rocks.

A fire truck helps firemen to
do their job.

A police car helps policemen and policewomen to do their job.

Some big tractors work to plow
fields.

Some small tractors work to
mow lawns.

Big boats are called ships and
carry many people.

Speedboats go fast and carry just a few people.

Some things to drive,

are just the right size for you!

 The end.

We hope you enjoyed this
Curious Toddler book.

Also in the Curious Toddler series...

Let's Learn About...Dogs!
Let's Learn About...Cats!
Let's Learn About...Things to Drive!
Let's Learn About...Jungle Animals!
Let's Learn About...Birds!
Let's Learn About...Wild Animals!
Let's Learn About...Horses!
Let's Learn About...Farm Animals!

ABOUT THE AUTHOR

Cheryl Shireman created the Curious Toddler Series. Cheryl is married and lives in Indiana on a beautiful lake with her husband. She has three grown children and one adorable granddaughter.

Cheryl also writes novels for big people:
Life is But a Dream: On The Lake
Life is But a Dream: In The Mountains
Broken Resolutions
Cooper Moon: The Calling

She is also the author of the beloved non-fiction book, You Don't Need a Prince: A Letter to My Daughter

All of her books can be found on Amazon and other retailers.
Her website is www.cherylshireman.com
She can also be found on Twitter and Facebook.

CPSIA information can be obtained
at www.ICGtesting.com
Printed in the USA
LVHW071743231218
601535LV00001B/4/P